The first-timer's cookbook

Principles, techniques & hidden secrets of the pros you can use to cook anything!

CHEF SHAWN BUCHER

The First-Timer's Cookbook
Chef Shawn Bucher

BookWise Publishing
65 E. Wadsworth Park Drive
Suite 110
Salt Lake City, Utah 84020
801 676-2420
www.bookwisewritewise.com

www.firsttimerscookbook.com

Cover Design by Garrett McFarland

Photography by Richard Brown

Book Design by Paul Killpack, Highland, Utah

Library of Congress Cataloging-in-Publication Data: Pending

The First-Timer's Cookbook / Shawn Bucher

ISBN 978-1-60645-008-6

First Printing

10 9 8 7 6 5 4 3 2 1

Printed in China

Introduction

Warning

You will have to learn to think for yourself if you're going to read this book. There, I said it. This book is not for someone who is looking for another collection of recipes. This is a book that will teach you how to look at food, decide what you want to do with it, and then do it. This is the book that *you start with* when learning, or re-learning, how to cook. This is the book that will lay the groundwork to enable you to create whatever you want.

The First Timer's Cookbook is all about the basics. It's for every person who wants to learn how to cook, from the newlywed bride—or groom—to the homemaker or career guy or gal, and every college kid out on their own for the first time who has ever said to themselves, "I wish I could cook." Although this is the ultimate beginner's crash course on the basic principles of cooking, you long-timer's might learn a thing or two as well. This is the book I wish I'd had when I started. Now, after working in and running professional kitchens for the last twelve years and training a lot of cooks, it's the book that I constantly use. It's also the one that I can refer people to read when they're either getting started or looking to learn a few new tricks.

Is this going to make you ready for your own Food Network show? Maybe not right away, but it will be a start. After reading this and practicing the concepts and principles (*practice is crucial*), you should be able to cook just about anything you can buy in the grocery store.

So, how am I going to show you how to cook?

Simply put, I'm going to show you how to use your most powerful asset when it comes to cooking, or anything really—your mind. Because after all, you know what you like, so let me just show you how to train your brain so you know how to get it.

First things first—keep it clean!

Before you start chopping, assembling or anything of the sort, remember to start, stay, and finish clean!

Why?

Because most cases of food poisoning are a result of people cooking in their own homes. That's right! We are actually making ourselves sick by not following the proper principles that will keep us safe.

Principles of Food Safety

1 Keep hot foods hot and cold foods cold. Avoid the "Danger Zone" between 40 and 140 degrees. Don't let foods stay in this area any longer than they have to. So if it's hot, hold it above 140 degrees, and if it's cold, keep it below 40 degrees.

2 Wash your hands with soap and warm water for at least twenty seconds before and after handling food. Bacteria can be spread all over your kitchen just by you not washing your hands properly. One way is to hum, whistle, or even sing your ABC's to yourself. This is a trick I use because from start to finish it usually takes about twenty seconds.

3 Don't cross-contaminate. Cross-contamination can occur when the bacteria transfer from one food to another through a shared surface. Don't let juices from raw meat, poultry or seafood come in contact with already-cooked foods or foods that will be eaten raw. For example, when you're cooking, don't put cooked meat on the same plate that held the raw meat. Also, don't cut carrots on the same cutting board you just used to trim the fat off the chicken breast.

4 Use the fridge to thaw items. Do not thaw meat, poultry or seafood on the kitchen counter. As a good rule, allow one day for every five pounds of weight. If you don't have time for this and you thaw in the microwave, then make sure to cook it as soon as possible. Whenever I thaw something, I always put a plate or something else underneath it to catch the juices so that if it does bleed, it will not get all over the fridge.

5 **Never leave meat or dairy products at room temperature for over three hours.** Your local health department will actually probably allow for up to four hours, but I say three hours to be on the safe side. Although it's a good idea to do this for all types of perishable food, it is crucial with meat and dairy products.

6 **Clean as you go.** Another tip to keep things tidy and to help you stay healthy is to clean as you go. Every chef that I have either worked under or with, always teaches their employees to do this. A professional kitchen moves very fast and there is no time for messing with clutter or for cleaning up after someone else.

So remember, whenever you are in the kitchen, keep it safe, clean and sanitary and clean as you go.

Foreword

Everyone who has ever wanted to learn how to cook has probably asked themselves the same question, "Where do I start?"

I'm sure many of you may have thought that by watching the *Food Network* and imitating your favorite chef's every move would make you a great cook. Or that if you read one of those nine-hundred page cookbooks that has all the ins and outs of cooking in it, you could cook anything. Maybe you thought that the more cookbooks you read and recipes you followed would naturally make you a pro.

But as you know, or found out, starting is the hardest part of learning to cook. And not having the right tools makes it even harder.

Realistically, who has time to watch twenty-four hours of the *Food Network* or time to shop for those ingredients the recipes call for? Plus, when you get that huge professional cookbook, you may look at it twice and then throw your hands up in frustration because you can't understand half of what they're talking about. Wouldn't it be nice to actually be able to cook and understand why you do things, not just make another recipe? Of course it would—that's what you wanted in the first place. So here is the place to start.

The First-Timer's Cookbook is the perfect beginner's cookbook. It's simple, easy to understand and has lots of pictures to help you start out right without being overwhelmed. This book could very easily be the foundation for every other cookbook you'll ever read.

When it comes to cooking, having the right tools makes all the difference. *The First-Timer's Cookbook* is a great tool, one to which you may find yourself referring back time and time again. It not only gives you a place to start but also provides a good foundation of skills, techniques and knowledge so that you have a way to go on to bigger and better things faster.

Now I can finally make what I want, not just what the recipe says.

—Richard Paul Evans
#1 *New York Times* bestselling author of *The Christmas Box*

Chapter 1
Menu Planning & Table Set-up

When planning a menu, most chefs will take into account many different things such as color, texture, how it will hold, etc. But for now, we're going to focus on the basics.

The easiest way to plan a meal is to focus on and establish three things: a protein, a vegetable and a starch.

If you're working in a food service setting you may also want to throw in a soup, salad and a dessert.

Most dining experiences will follow the order and format of: appetizer, soup and/or salad, entrée, and dessert.

Protein—These include chicken, fish, veal, mutton, or beef. They may also be items such as tofu. Proteins are primarily main course focus items. Now when I say main course, I'm talking about things like turkey or roast beef, items that are the general focus. For example, if you were to ask someone what they were having for dinner, then you probably would hear a response of something like "turkey" or "roast beef," usually not things like "zucchini," or "carrots," unless you're a vegetarian or just having vegetables.

Vegetable—A great, and probably the healthiest part of any meal, is the vegetables. These are items such as squash, broccoli, carrots, corn, etc. They are usually not the focal point of the menu, but more of an accent. They add a nice color and balance to almost any menu.

Starch—Whether it is a traditional starch such as potatoes, rice or pasta, starch is a pivotal part of any meal. This is what sticks to your ribs, fills you up and provides you with the carbohydrates and energy you need.

By just focusing on making the best protein, vegetable and starch, you will be on your way to making wonderful meals time and time again. Then as you get the basic steps down, you'll be able to move on from there.

Most dining experiences will follow the order and format of appetizer, soup and/or salad, entrée, and dessert.

Table Set-up

A table set-up can be as simple or as extravagant as you like. Here are some standard rules for setting a table.

Step 1

A dinner plate goes in the center of each of the place settings.

Step 2

The larger fork, or dinner fork, goes to the left of the plate and the smaller fork, or salad fork, goes to the left of the larger fork.

Step 3

The salad plate goes to the left of the forks.

Step 4

The knife goes to the right of the plate with the sharp edge facing toward the plate.

Step 5

If you are serving both soup and dessert, put the dessert spoon (usually smaller) to the right of the knife. Then place the soup spoon to the right of the dessert spoon.

Step 6

The bread plate, or B&B (bread and butter) plate, is set with a butter knife just above the forks. For an informal to semi-formal setting, I recommend just using the dinner knife.

Step 7

The water glass goes just above the knife. If you are serving wine, put the wine glass just to the right of the water glass.

By just focusing on making the best protein, vegetable and starch, you will be on your way to making wonderful meals time and time again.

Step 8

If you decide to serve coffee, place the saucer to the right of the forks and place the cup on top of the saucer. You may also place a small spoon to the right of the cup on the saucer for stirring the coffee.

Step 9

Last, put a folded napkin in the center of each plate.

If you forget where something goes, just remember that the table is set so that you work your way in. If you have salad before the main course, the salad fork goes on the outside of the dinner fork. If you have soup before dessert, the soup spoon goes on the outside of the dessert spoon. So don't get confused. Just think, "What are we going to eat first?"

Chapter 2
Getting Started

Make sure everything that goes into the mixture is laid out on the counter/table or within a few feet of your work area before you begin so all you have to do is grab it, instead of searching for it.

Before you begin cooking anything, it's always good to have everything ready. If you are making a stew or a soup, make sure the onions and carrots are cut up prior to you turning on the flame or element on which you're going to be cooking. This way you don't have to run around the kitchen looking for everything only to find that you are out of something you need as everything else burns on the stove.

Make sure everything that goes into the mixture is laid out on the counter or table or within a few feet of your work area.

Chapter 3
Cookware—Your Tools

An important element of being ready to cook is surrounding yourself with your cookware or cooking tools. Pots, pans, bowls, knives and various other utensils constitute your tools.

Cookware is un-ending. New tools and gadjets come on the market everyday that either replace an old tool or have an entirely new function that makes cooking easier and more time and cost-effective. You'll never have every tool out there; you may never even hear about most of them. Just remember to experiment and try things out. If you see something you think might work well for you, then go for it. It never hurts to try something new.

These are a few of the universal tools that you'll use most often.

Thermometer

- Thermometer—not only to help with food safety, but it also enables you to cook things to the correct temperature, i.e. perfectly (most of the time)

- Mixing bowls

- Spatulas (offset, regular and bowl scrapers)

- Pots—what you are used to seeing soups, sauces, vegetables, macaroni and cheese, and so forth cooked in

Mixing Bowls

- Colanders or strainers—used primarily to strain water and wash vegetables, etc.

- Basic utensils—knife, fork, spoon

- Cooking pans (glass or aluminum)

- Whisks—designed for mixing items thoroughly

- Knives

- Electric tools (blender, mixer)

Spatula

- Measuring cups—universal measuring tools so your ingredients are in the same amounts as given in the recipe

- Cutting boards—these provide cutting surfaces so you don't damage your countertops

These tools are basically everything you will need. Of course there are hundreds of other tools out there, but as I said, these are what you will use most of the time.

Whisk

Measuring Cups

Cutting Boards

Knives

Chapter 4
Knives & Knife Skills

I know this may come as a surprise to some of you out there, but you are going to have to learn to use a knife. This is the fun part. You're going to learn how to really handle a knife and never cut yourself.

First, there are a lot of different knives out there. Second, you're never going to learn to use all of them, or even most of them. Try out a few and you'll end up just going back to the same one or two for almost everything you do. This is where experience and trial and error come into play. You may like to use some knives for things that they may not be primarily designed for and that's alright, because it's *your* kitchen.

For example, I like to use my cleaver to cut up vegetables like zucchini, squash, carrots and celery. But then I like to use my chef's knife to break down and quarter whole chickens. This is a basic role reversal of the two knives, since cleavers are designed to break down meat and bones and a chef's knife is used to cut vegetables. But that's what I like to do because it's comfortable for me.

Part of learning is growing, so after doing a little cooking and refining your skills you may find yourself looking to broaden your spectrum and begin using a larger array of knives. But if you're like most cooks, you will probably always come back to one knife in particular, the chef's knife (or French knife). The chef's knife is the most versatile of all the knives and is probably the one that everyone is most familiar with. Most people in professional kitchens will use these knives ninety-five percent of the time or more because of their versatility.

No matter what knife you use, knife skills are basically the same and come down to this–don't cut yourself.

If you watch your mom or grandmother cut things like potatoes, vegetables or meat with a knife, you may think that it looks safe enough since they're not cutting themselves each time. But then you watch a professional chef slice up an onion in half the time it takes your mom, all while keeping their fingers right next to the blade. You may think to yourself, "How do they keep their fingers so close and cut it so fast and not cut themselves?"

No matter what knife you use, knife skills are basically the same and come down to this–don't cut yourself.

Right Way

Wrong Way

Use a damp cloth or a rubber mat

You know from watching your mom or grandmother, if they were to go that fast, cutting the way that they do, they would definitely be losing some fingers. Just remember, the reason your mom cuts the way she does is because Grandma showed her. And the reason that Grandma cuts the way she does, is because Great-Grandma showed her. Cooking is an essential skill that almost everyone at one time or another has wanted to master at some level. So when we want to learn how to do something, we look to those who are there who already know how and we emulate them. Good recipes can travel through a family for decades. But so can bad habits formed through ignorance.

You know that if your mom knew a better, faster way, she would show you. But if she doesn't, then look to those who do.

Always keep your fingers and thumb out of harm's way by keeping them back and letting your fingers guide your knife.

If you follow this rule you will not cut yourself. One of the first chefs I ever worked for told me this and I did not believe him until after I cut the tip off of my finger for the second time. Then I really started to listen.

Keep your blade against your knuckles so that you know that your hand is out of harm's way. By using your knuckles as guides you will always have a bearing on the knife. This is how the chefs you see on TV can always look at the camera instead what they are cutting. They know exactly where their knife is at all times. They are constantly in contact with the blade and know that their fingers are safe if they folllow this method.

When you think of knives I'm sure that you probably also think of cutting boards, since the two are used almost like salt and pepper—you can't have one without the other.

So here is a neat little trick to keep your cutting board from moving too much on you while you are cutting.

Put a damp cloth or towel underneath the board. With that layer of friction between the cutting board and the counter top, the board won't move nearly as much as if you didn't have it there. You can also buy plastic, washable mats that are designed for keeping cutting boards in place.

This is just another way of making things safer and easier.

Chapter 5
Cooking Procedures

Most cooking procedures involve heat. We use that heat to raise the internal temperature of items that we cook to a certain level, killing microorganisms and making it safe to eat.

Through experience and trial and error we have learned that not all cooking procedures are created equal, but they each have their place. Almost everyone is familiar with dishes like roasted or grilled chicken, but what do they mean? Do you know the difference? Most of us probably do, but let's look at how we apply the different methods and why and when we use them. Then we will also see why it can sometimes be beneficial to use multiple cooking methods for just one item.

There are two main cooking methods—dry or moist.

Moist Heat
Poach, Simmer, Boil, Steam, Braise

Boiling

Boiling is what happens to water when you turn the heat all the way up and the liquid in the pot bubbles or boils. Usually you only use this method of cooking for things such as pastas. If you were to cook meat like this, it would usually come out tough because it cooks too quickly and doesn't allow the time needed for the protein in the meat to be broken down and tenderized.

So how do you boil water or any other liquid? Get the pot, one that will fit what you are cooking, and add the liquid. Then place the pot on the heating element and turn the element all the way up to high. Then let the liquid heat until it is rapidly boiling.

Simmering

Simmering is how most foods cooked in liquid are done. This is how soups and sauces are cooked—in a gentle bubble, versus the rapidly agitated bubbling action of boiling.

It's sometimes beneficial to use multiple cooking methods for just one item.

Bring things to a simmer much like you would a boil, only turn the element up almost all the way, instead of all the way to high. Then adjust your heat accordingly, turning it up or down as needed until the liquid is simmering.

Poaching

Poaching is cooking with the water or liquid very hot, but not bubbling. This is a way to cook very delicate foods like eggs and fish.

Braising

Braising is when you sear something to lock in the moisture and then finish cooking it in a little bit of liquid without actually covering it all the way in the liquid. An example of searing would be to put a piece of meat on a very hot skillet or grill to brown it. This basically is the combination of the dry heat method of grilling and the moist heat method of simmering.

Tips for Success with These Methods

It is important to note that most of the moist cooking methods start with you bringing the liquid to a boil first. The reason this is done is that when you introduce your meat, potatoes or vegetables to the hot liquid, these ingredients immediately cool the temperature of the water so that it is no longer boiling. From there you may adjust the temperature accordingly.

Steaming

Steaming is when you cook food using direct steam. This is usually done by using a specialized machine called a steamer, but it may also be done by placing a little bit of water in the bottom of a pot and putting the food into the pot. This way the food is not completely covered, but is still exposed to the hot steam. Steaming is a lot like boiling because the food is cooked at the same temperature—212 degrees Fahrenheit—but without the agitation of bubbles all around it. Although steaming cooks at the same temperature as boiling, it actually carries a lot more heat and cooks items very rapidly. You probably don't realize it, but you actually use steam to cook potatoes wrapped in foil. All you are doing is heating the natural moisture in the potato and trapping it inside the foil so you are actually *steaming* a *baked* potato. So even though you are essentially steaming the potato, it is called a baked potato because you are baking it in the oven.

Dry heat
Grill, Broil, Roast, Bake, Sauté, Fry

Grilling/Broiling

Most of us associate summertime cooking with things like the barbecue. This is probably one of the most popular of all the cooking methods because of the unique flavor and the showmanship associated with it. But it is also one of the most misunderstood cooking methods.

Grilling is based on the principle of intense heat rising from beneath the cooking surface. A lot of times when we refer to grilling, we actually mean what is known as charbroiling. The barbecue grill that you use in your backyard is actually a charbroiler. Both a grill and a charbroiler are based on the same principle of intense heat rising from below to cook or grill an item. But the most noticeable difference is that a charbroiler leaves the distinctive lines on the items being cooked. A grill will generally leave a light brown mark on the entire surface of the item being cooked since the item being cooked is laying flat on the surface. On the grill, the item's entire surface is in contact with the surface of the grill. That's why when you flip a pancake, it cooks evenly, since only one side of the item can touch the grill at a time.

When you are charbroiling an item, the only part of the charbroiler actually touching the item is the slats; these slats are what leave the distinctive grilling marks. On the other hand, the other source of heat comes from between the slats, from the heat below.

This is how broiling works. The flame beneath heats up the slats to very high temperatures, as well as putting out tremendous amounts of heat between the slats, so not only are you putting your food on a direct heat source—the hot slats—but also an indirect heat—the heat from between the slats.

Because temperatures are so high and the heat is so direct, this is a very harsh cooking method. One of the drawbacks of grilling or broiling is the fact that the outside of your items are subjected to this very harsh heat, while the inside takes longer to heat. A lot of times, this causes you to burn the outside while trying to get the inside to cook all the way.

How to Grill Perfectly

Have you ever wondered why when you go to a good restaurant the meat seems to be perfectly done on the outside and on the inside?

Here's the secret.

Most, if not all professional kitchens, will actually "mark" meat beforehand by putting it on the grill or broiler just to get the marks and that unique flavor, but will not cook it all the way right then. Instead, just before service, they will put the meat in the oven, ensure that it is cooked to the proper temperature (also making it possible to cook multiple items at once) and then serve it. This way, meat can be cooked to the exact temperature the patron wants without having to constantly watch it to prevent burning the outside. This does wonders for meats such as chicken which is very easy to overcook on a grill or broiler.

So if this method works for professional cooks, it can also work for you.

Roasting/Baking

When you think of roasting, you probably think of roasted chicken or roasted potatoes or roasted leg of lamb. To roast something is to surround it with hot, dry air. Baking is doing the same thing, except that when you bake you are generally referring to foods like breads and cakes. So if you're putting something like meat in the oven, then you're roasting it. If it's a cake, you're baking it. Then there are potatoes which can be referred to as either baked or roasted. Confusing, isn't it? Just remember that the words roasting or baking are essentially interchangeable.

Sauté

Sauté means to cook very quickly in a small amount of butter, oil or some other kind of fat. This method is designed to soften the texture and get the flavors out of whatever you are cooking. So when you imagine someone cooking like this, they are usually tossing the mixture rapidly so it doesn't burn because the temperatures are so high.

You will use this method often when making soups and sauces. It's also a popular way of cooking vegetables.

As I mentioned before, this is a signature cooking method. When photographs are taken, there is usually a chef holding a pan tossing some sort of concoction high in the air over a large flame. Let me assure you, it's not just a show, there is a method to this madness.

While working at a restaurant, I had so many things going on during a busy rush period that I would literally need one of my hands doing one thing and my other hand doing something else. It was that busy. So instead of having to pick up a spatula or spoon to stir the mixture, therefore using both hands for one task, I could actually use my left hand to toss the mix in the pan, while I would flip the chicken or steak on the broiler.

Now, are you going to be in a similar situation where you need the use of both hands? Maybe not in the same capacity that I was, but it is a good skill to learn because you never know when you might want to use it.

Frying

All I have would have to say is French fries and everyone would know what kind of cooking method I am talking about. Even though French fries are usually "deep" fried, which is completely submerging the item in the fat or oil, it is the same concept.

If sautéing is cooking something quickly in a small amount of fat, then just increase the amount of fat and you've got frying. They're both some of the very fastest cooking methods. Why? Because fat (butter, oil, etc.) has a lower boiling point than water, therefore it heats up a lot faster and, subsequently, cooks hotter and faster.

Chapter 6
How to Cook Beef, Lamb & Pork

To be successful in any cooking endeavor and especially when cooking any meat, always begin with the end in mind. How do you want the meat to taste and look? Do you want it to fall apart in your mouth, or be more flavorfully distinct like a steak? Or maybe you want both. The first step in this process is finding the right cut of meat and understanding why it is right for what you are trying to accomplish.

One of the secrets to cooking great meats is starting with a great product. This goes for everything that you cook but especially any kind of meat. In cooking beef, lamb, poultry, pork or fish, **fresh is always best.**

The secret to cooking great meats is starting with a great product. This goes for everything you cook but especially with meat.

Grades of Meat

The basic meat scale is graded by the following.

Description	Beef	Lamb	Pork & Chicken
Most expensive, highest quality, served in high establishments.	Prime	Prime	(not graded, inspected for safety)
Good quality, generally used in most food service, some grocery.	Choice	Choice	
Limited marbling, cheaper meat, usually used in grocery stores.	Select	Good	

As you can see, the meat that you purchase in grocery stores is generally not the highest quality. The higher quality meats are generally sold at a much higher price to food service institutions. You can always request a better cut of meat from your grocer, but you will pay a much higher price. That's why most grocers stay in the "select" or "good" ranges—because of the price.

Now you know another secret to how restaurants and hotels make those meals that you just can't quite make the same at home.

Getting the Right Cut

Another tip to cooking meats is choosing the right cut for the right recipe. Steaks are good for grilling/broiling, whereas roasts are good for roasting.

When you choose a steak, the T-bones, Porterhouses and Rib Eye steaks are more expensive than the Top Sirloins because of marbling and fat content. That's also why these steaks are so much better-tasting too, because of this built-in flavor.

You probably won't want to roast a steak because that's not the best way to cook that cut of meat. Roasts and larger cuts of meat are need "roasting" for the longer cooking times and less intense temperatures.

Buying Meat

Meat should have the following characteristics when purchasing it:

- No offensive odors
- Nice, bright color
- No discoloration spots
- Firm, yet mancuverable

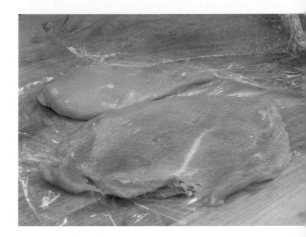

Cooking Meat

When cooking meat, dry heat procedures give you options of rare, medium and well done. Moist cooking procedures are always well done.

Moist Heat

If you're cooking using a moist procedure, you can tell when the meat is done by the tenderness versus the temperature. When the meat is done, it is way past well done temperature wise. The tenderness comes with long, slow cooking times, not high temperatures. Stay in the 250 to 300 degree range on your oven, otherwise you will cook the meat too fast and it may cause it to become tough.

Dry Heat

There are two methods to gauge dry cooking methods—by touch or by temperature.

Touch is the preferred method among most restaurant cooks, mainly because it's fast and effective, especially if you have a lot of experience doing it.

How to Measure by Touch

Rare feels soft and gives to pressure, but not as much as raw meat.

Medium is firmer and more resilient and springs back readily after being pressed.

Well done is firm and does not give to pressure.

How to Measure with Temperature

If you would like to be more accurate, and if you're just starting out, then measure by temperature.

To help you with this, do what the chefs do—test it with a meat thermometer. Buy one at most grocery stores for a few dollars. Then just follow the instructions on the package and you're ready to go.

The following chart will help you know when it's done.

Internal Temperatures of items when they're done (Fahrenheit)			
Pork	165-170 degrees		
	Rare	Medium Rare	Well Done
Beef	130 degrees	140-145 degrees	160 degrees
Lamb	130 degrees	145 degrees	160 degrees

You probably noticed that pork is only given one internal temperature. That's because pork harbors a little parasite which causes Trichinosis, a foodborne illness that can make you extremely sick. That's why pork is cooked well done.

After having explained a little about temperatures, let me just say that you can overcook things. When you do, they are dry, the texture is poor and it just doesn't taste as good.

One of the biggest problems in cooking meat is making it too dry and/or too tough. That's because people cook meat at temperatures too high and for too long. When protein cooks, it coagulates or tightens up, losing moisture. That's why restaurants and hotels simply "mark" their steaks and other meats to give them the flavor they want and then finish them in the oven. By taking the meat off the grill or broiler and finishing it in the oven, you alleviate the time that the meat is subjected to the harsh, dry, direct heat of the broiler or grill, thus lowering the temperature and time.

Fat or marbling is also a very important thing to understand. Marbling is the fat lines you see throughout the meat, not the big chunks of stuff on the outside of the meat. That is plain old fat.

Marbling is the fat that is responsible for most of the meat's flavor and juiciness. It also makes it easier to chew, since it breaks up the muscle fibers.

One of the ways in which fat or marbling gives meat its flavor is by "smoking." When you place a piece of meat on a broiler and the heat begins to increase the internal temperature of the meat, the fat begins to melt and drip into the fire. This is called reaching its "smoke point." When the fat hits the coals or charcoal, it smokes and then rises into the meat, giving the meat its distinct, smoky flavor.

This brings me to a little known principle that will help you *not* overcook meats. It's called carry-over cooking.

Carry-Over Cooking

When you pull something out of the oven or off the grill or broiler, the internal temperature continues to rise because the outside of the meat is hotter than the inside. The temperature will continue to rise until the heat is evenly dispersed throughout the meat. This is called carry-over cooking because, even though it's out of the oven, the meat is still cooking. This is something you need to remember because if you want a roast at 140 degrees, don't pull it out of the oven at 140. If you do, the internal temperature will rise and you will end up with a roast that is really ten to fifteen degrees higher, causing the roast to be "overdone." Instead, pull the meat out at 130 degrees and let the principle of carry-over cooking work in your favor.

The Secret to Cooking Perfect Meats with Carry-Over Cooking

Each meat has a different carry-over cooking time, but the biggest factor in determining when to pull something out of the oven or off the stove or grill is how big it is. As I mentioned in the previous example, for larger cuts of meat, like roasts, the solution to not overcooking it is to pull it out of the oven ten to fifteen degrees below where you want it and let it sit for fifteen to thirty minutes. This allows the meat to essentially finish cooking and also allows the meat to hold on to some of those juices that make it so moist. If you cut the meat immediately after taking it out of the oven, you tend to lose moisture which leads to dryer meat.

For smaller portions, use shorter times. So if you are cooking five four-ounce chicken breasts, pull them out of the oven or off the grill when they are closer to two to three degrees below where you want them and only let them sit for three to five minutes.

An important thing to remember is that the internal temperature of items such as chicken must be raised above 165 degrees to ensure no salmonella or other harmful bacteria that can hurt you. So if you want it done to 165, pulling it out or off at 165 or even 167 is just fine. Since the carry-over cooking time is so small, it won't make that much of a difference. The meat will still be juicy and it's better to be safe than sorry.

Chapter 7
How to Cook Poultry

Characteristics and Differences of Poultry

When discussing poultry, I'll be talking mostly about chicken and turkey, the most commonly used types of poultry.

Some of the differences between meats like beef, pork and poultry have to do with the maturity. While beef tends to get better after a proper aging process, the younger the bird the better. Young birds have softer, more tender flesh, while older birds tend to be tougher and require slower, longer cooking periods.

Light and Dark Meat

There is also the most widely known distinction in the poultry category itself—light and dark meat.

Light meat is found mostly in the breast and wings. This meat has less fat, less connective tissue such as tendons and ligaments and cooks faster than dark meat does.

Dark meat is the opposite—it has higher fat content and more connective tissue, thus needing longer cooking times. Dark meat is found in the legs and thighs of the birds.

Buying Poultry

These are some characteristics to look for when purchasing fresh poultry:

- No strong odors
- Light color
- No red or brown discoloration spots on meat
- Somewhat firm and not saggy or mushy

Young birds have softer, more tender flesh, while older birds tend to be tougher and require slower, longer cooking periods.

Cooking Poultry

Poultry is very versatile and can be cooked following any of the mentioned cooking procedures. It is generally cheaper than most beef, lamb or pork and is also one of the healthiest choices of all proteins, since most of the fat is trimmed off and there is no marbling like there is in beef.

You can very easily overcook poultry, especially in cooking procedures such as grilling or broiling. Overcooking poultry makes it extremely dry and "chalky" tasting.

When cooking poultry there are some universal factors, techniques and tips to be aware of:

1 Any poultry is always cooked to at least 165 degrees.

2 When cooking a larger bird such as a large chicken or turkey, use a thermometer to check the internal temperature. When the bird is done, it should be around 180 degrees. Always measure the temperature in the thigh (dark meat section), since this is generally the last area cooked.

3 Another way to gauge how long it will take to cook is to remember fifteen minutes per pound. So if you have a three pound chicken, check the temperature after forty-five minutes of cooking. If it's a fifteen pound turkey, check the temperature after three hours and forty-five minutes.

4 Poultry is done when:

- Juices are running clear, instead of red or pink
- Joints are loose and flesh is beginning to fall off bone
- Meat feels firm to the touch

Remember that when you're cooking items such as chicken breasts or thighs, you should usually only have to cook them for 25 to 35 minutes at a temperature of 350 degrees or higher. This is usually plenty of time for the internal temperature to reach 165 degrees and for the meat to not be overcooked. But once again, use your thermometer to make sure.

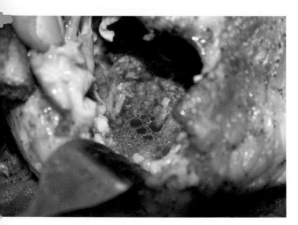

Not clear, not done

Basting

One of the techniques mostly associated with cooking poultry is basting. To baste a turkey or chicken, simply pour or "paint" the juices that are coming off the bird over the top of it to help remoisten the flesh. This is generally done when roasting or baking the poultry.

An Important Tip

Because poultry is one of the more volatile meats (it spoils easily and is known to harbor a harmful bacteria known as salmonella), it's important to use care and caution when dealing with it.

If you are going to be using poultry in a stew, soup or sauce, always try to cook it first before adding it to any mixture. This will help to eliminate any possibility of cross-contaminating the other food in the mix.

Raw, not done

Done

Chapter 8
How to Cook Fish

Fish is very much like other meats. We eat the muscle tissue of the fish which is made up of the same things as red meat and poultry (water, protein, fat and some vitamins and minerals). But there is almost no connective tissue in fish which makes it very different from red meat and poultry. This major difference also causes it to:

- Cook much faster than other meats
- And it's naturally tender

When purchasing fresh fish, make sure that the following traits are present:

- No "fishy" smell or strong odor
- Nice bright color with no discolored spots

Once again, fresh is always best, especially when it comes to fish. Anyone who says that they don't like seafood has never had *good* seafood. A lot of what people get in grocery stores has been frozen and thawed a couple of times and has a very strong and distinct fishy smell and taste when cooked. Frozen seafood is not always like this, but a lot of times it is. In my experience, fresh seafood rarely tastes "fishy," and really is the only way to go.

Differences in Fish—Fat versus Lean

The major difference in fish is the fat content. Some examples are:

Lean Fish	Fat Fish
Halibut	Salmon
Sole	Trout
Cod	Swordfish
Tilapia	Tuna

An easy way to remember which is which is to remember *light is white*. This rule applies since the leaner fish when cooked turn lighter and appear white instead of an off-white or translucent color when they are raw.

> *What people get in grocery stores has been frozen and thawed a couple of times and has a very strong and distinct fishy smell and taste.*

Cooking Fish

As mentioned before, fish cooks very quickly and is usually flaky when done.

Since lean fish has very little fat content, it usually needs to have some sort of fat added such as butter or oil. This aids in the taste and helps protect it from drying out, especially when using a dry heat method such as grilling/broiling or baking/roasting.

An easy way to skin the fish is after cooking one side, turn and simply peel

Baking

The best fish for baking is a fatty-type fish since they don't dry out as much. Whether it is a fat fish or lean fish, you will probably still want to baste it with butter or oil so that you run less chance of it drying out.

Fish is much like other kinds of meat in that the biggest problem is overcooking. Fish usually doesn't take much more than ten to fifteen minutes to cook if you're baking it or five to ten minutes if you're grilling it.

Broiling/Grilling

Once again, fat fish is best for this cooking method because of the drying out factor. A trick to cooking a lean fish this way is to coat it in flour before placing it on the grill. This forms a thin crust and helps to lock in the moisture. You may also fully bread the fish, a process we will refer to in Chapter #10.

Broiling fish is very difficult because it cooks so fast. Placing it on some sort of flat surface that acts like a skillet or grill will enable you to cook it on the broiler, without it breaking up and falling through the broiler slats. There is nothing I hate more than a perfectly cooked piece of fish that falls through the slats as I try to take it off.

Another way to do it is to just leave the skin on the fish so that it acts like a piece of tape that holds it together. Then when it's done, just peel the skin off (it comes off very easily) or if it's a trout, then just eat the skin too. It's actually very good and all that Omega 3 is definitely good for you.

Steaming

Fish is a great candidate for this method of cooking since it cooks so fast.

Steam is a harsh way to cook something compared to other moist heat methods since the temperatures are so intense. So be very mindful when using this method that you don't overcook the fish, because it's very easy to do.

For example, if it were to take 15 minutes to cook in the oven, it would only take 7 to 10 minutes to steam. However, if you overcook the fish by steaming it, it also doesn't dry out the same. If you look at a piece of over-baked fish, you can tell it is dry but you probably won't be able to tell if you've over-steamed the fish until you take a bite.Both will taste the same—chalky and powdery—but they'll look different.

Chapter 9
Preparing & Cooking Vegetables

Vegetables are essentially edible parts of plants. They come in all shapes and sizes, textures and colors. When it comes to cooking, vegetables are not much different than meats. You can cook them using all of the same cooking methods and the same rules apply. They can also be seasoned the same, stored the same, even served the same, although most of the time they are there to complement a meal rather than to be the center focus.

When cooking vegetables, a good rule to remember is that the softer the vegetable is, the quicker it's going to cook, regardless of how you cook it.

Vegetables are difficult to gauge because you can't really use temperature to tell when they're done as effectively as you can when you judge by the look and feel. But of course, some general rules apply.

Steaming/Simmering

You can never go wrong with moist heat when cooking vegetables. This is how I personally cook vegetables 99% of the time. Whether it's steaming or simmering, this is the quickest, most efficient way to do it.

Most of you reading this will think, "I know that," or "I do that already." Even though you might already use this method of cooking, chances are you are "over" doing it. That's right, once again the biggest problem I have seen with vegetables is overcooking. So here is a way to tell when your vegetables are done.

Most vegetables are perfectly done when they are bright in color and still somewhat firm. So when the color starts to get duller and the texture mushier, they are becoming too done, or overdone. You might like vegetables overdone and mushy, but as a chef, I always adhere to the standard of cooking them to the point that they are brightly colored and not mushy.

So which one's right? The answer, whatever you want. Why? Because it's your kitchen and you can cook however you want it, but if you come into my kitchen, you're getting bright, crisp, firm veggies, none of that mushy stuff.

Most vegetables are perfectly done when they are bright in color and still somewhat firm.

31

A Tip to Getting Perfectly Done Vegetables

This trick is especially good when you're making some sort of cold vegetable dish or preparing vegetables ahead of time.

Since vegetables contain a lot of water, once you get that water hot, it's hard to cool down immediately. The carry-over cooking time is longer on vegetables because of this. So when you cook your vegetables perfectly, and you want them to stay that way, shock them.

Shocking Vegetables

To do this, simply take them out of the hot water and run them under cold water. This cools them down to a point that they will stop cooking and stay the way you want them.

If you're serving the vegetables hot, you can still shock them, just don't cool them down all the way. Instead of running them under cold water for thirty seconds, just do it for five seconds. This keeps them hot enough but slows down the cooking process as well.

Grilling/Broiling

When undertaking this method of cooking, keep in mind three things. First, use some sort of fat or oil so the vegetables won't stick. Second, remember the principle of carry-over cooking will be a factor here. And third, you can't go wrong with just seasoning them with salt and pepper.

Step 1

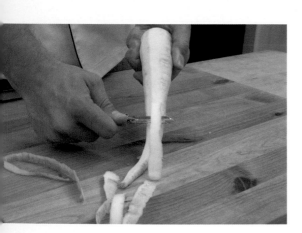

Vegetables love to stick to the pan, grill or broiler they're being cooked on so some sort of fat or oil will help prevent this. I generally use butter because I like the flavor it gives to the vegetables. Some recipes call for either olive or canola oil. It really just comes down to what you like, what flavor you want them to have, etc.

Step 2

When you take the veggies off the hot surface, remember that you have just started them cooking, and with all that moisture that they have locked up inside, they're going to keep steaming themselves long after they are out of the heat.

Step 3

The classic seasonings—salt and pepper—bring out the natural flavors so nicely that I usually just leave it at that. Why mess with tried and true winner?

Cooking in Conjunction with Vegetables

When I first started in the kitchen, I was introduced to a combination that changed my life. I would never make a soup, sauce or cook meat the same again. That combination is onions, carrots and celery. These are the "salt and pepper" of vegetables that make bad things good and good things great.

I almost always start with this combo that the French call *mirepoix (pronounced meer-ah-pwa)* whenever I roast something in the oven or make a soup.

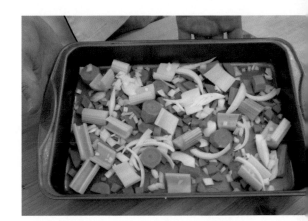

When roasting something like a chicken, turkey or beef roast, I put an equal amount of onion, carrot and celery on the bottom of the pan and then place the meat on top. Not only does it give it a little added flavor, but the moisture from the vegetables helps the meat to come out more tender and moist.

Sauces and soups begin in the same way many times with equal amounts of onions, carrots and celery to give them a little extra goodness.

Preparing Fruits and Vegetables

Vegetables and fruits are a major part, or should be, of our diets. Next I'll discuss some of the commonly used fruits and vegetables along with some of the more common ways to clean and prepare them. I have also included some tips with a few of them, but the tip that applies to them all universally is to make sure that they are washed well before using them.

Apples

Apples come in many different colors, sizes and even flavors. Different apples are used for different things, but you can clean them all the same.

Stand the apple up and cut it in half.

Cut a triangle shape out by taking one half of the apple and cut on a slant into the white flesh near the core, not quite all the way through. Then flip the apple half and make the same cut on the opposite side.

Asparagus

I have always loved asparagus. It's easy to prepare, is great for presentation and has a very unique taste. Most often you will find it in bunches in the grocery. Many times you will see the asparagus bunches stored
standing in a shallow pool of water. This allows it to continue to stay moist. If the asparagus doesn't have the water, it starts to dry out, which makes the stalk tougher than it naturally is.

To prepare the asparagus, simply cut off about the last quarter of the base of the stalk. The bottom portion is usually lighter. You only want the nice, dark green portion. The end portion of the vegetable is a little tougher and can be somewhat "woody" tasting. That's why you remove it.

I leave the rubber bands on both ends until after I have cut it, making it more manageable and
allowing for quicker cleanup since you can just discard the ends in one bunch.

Avocado

Avocados can be used in a lot of dishes. As the base for guacamole and a key ingredient in many other dishes, avocados are very versatile.

First, remove the stem.

Cut the avocado in half lengthwise by running the knife around the hard pit in the center.

Take the knife and swiftly hit middle of the pit with the middle of the knife. This will allow you to remove the pit. Simply twist the knife to remove the pit.

When the pit has been removed, simply slide a spoon into each half and scoop the green flesh out.

Bell Peppers

As you can see bell peppers come in many different colors. They all taste the same but vary in price. The green bell peppers are the cheapest, the red ones are a little more expensive and the yellow and orange are much more expensive. The only real difference is the color.

There are a few ways to clean a bell pepper. I have seen probably at least three or four different ways, but I'm going to focus on the two primary methods that I have seen most commonly used here.

Method One

Start by standing the pepper up with the stem at the top.

Slice the side of the pepper by starting at the top just to the side of the stem. Then make three more similar slices until you are left with just the seeds and internal white part and the four sides you just sliced.

Now turn the stem and seed portion on its side and slice off the bottom green part. Then discard the seeds and stem.

If there is too much of the soft, white internal part left on the sides you can easily remove it with your fingers.

Method Two

Start by standing the pepper up with the stem at the top as before.

Cut the pepper right down the middle so that you have two equal parts.

Simply grab the core and pull it out with your fingers. Remove the rest of the white part and discard it.

Now that the pepper has been cleaned, you can slice, or "julienne," the sides into thin strips. Lay the whole side with the skin side down and guide your knife gently through, using your fingers as a guide to help make the strips uniform in size. The reason you lay it skin side down, is because it's much easier to cut through the inside fleshy part of the pepper instead of the tough protective outer skin.

If you want to "dice" these strips up into a much smaller size, simply take the strips you just cut and turn them so that you are cutting across them, making them into small cubes or small squares.

Broccoli

Broccoli is another versatile vegetable. It is commonly used in soups because of its unique flavor, or in various vegetable mixes for its color and texture—and it's is great all by itself, too.

Broccoli is usually kept in bunches, just remove the rubber band and separate the pieces to get started.

Remove the little green leaves by just pulling them off with your fingers. These little green leaves have a bitter taste so discard them.

Next cut the top part of the broccoli, called the "floret," from the stem. Cook the floret as one large piece or cut it into smaller pieces to allow for faster cooking.

Most people will discard the stem, but I think that the stem is one of the best parts of the broccoli. Leave the outside layer on or use a vegetable peeler or knife to remove it since it is a little tough. Now slice it and cook it along with the florets.

Carrots & Root Vegetables

Carrots are one of the most common vegetables and are commonly eaten hot and cold just like celery and other vegetables. Carrots are a root vegetable so the technique to cleaning and preparing them can also apply other root vegetables like parsnips.

Peel the outside layer of the carrot or root vegetable off using a vegetable peeler.

After the carrot is peeled, cut off the large stem.

Cut the carrot in half lengthwise.

Next you may cut the carrot a few different ways depending on what you're using it for. Cut it into large slices to use in a stew by slicing the halves.

Or cut it into "matchstick" pieces by slicing the halves and use them for relish/vegetable trays.

Can the "matchstick" slices down even further to use in soups or sauces.

Celery

Celery can be served hot or cold. It is used in cooking served hot, but is also an integral part of things like vegetable trays and served cold.

Cut off the base. This will release all the stems.

Cut off the bitter leaves and unusable tops.

Slice the stems into smaller pieces by following the next steps.

Cut each stem lengthwise into smaller parts. You may even cut these stems in the middle, making them into "matchsticks." These are the celery sticks you generally see served with Buffalo wings or on a vegetable tray.

Or dice the celery into small sizes for use in soups and sauces.

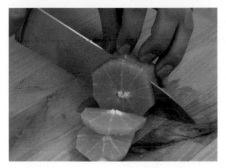

Citrus

Citrus fruits include oranges, lemons, limes, and grapefruit. They can be prepared by just slicing, peeling off the skin and eating them plain, cutting them in half and eating the juicy insides.

When juicing the fruit, there is one technique you can use before you actually cut into the fruit. Roll it on a hard surface before you cut it. This will loosen the membranes on the inside, making it easier for the juice to come out.

Cucumbers

Cucumbers may be served with or without the skin. Most restaurants will serve cucumbers without the skin since the skin many times has a bitter taste. To do this, simply peel the outside of the cucumber off with a vegetable peeler, just as you would a potato.

Whether you are serving the cucumber with or without the skin, there are a few different ways to cut them. Some ways include de-seeding them, but I will focus on the two quickest, most basic ways here.

Start by cutting off only one stem end because you'll end up slicing the entire cucumber, eventually coming to the end, at which point you can discard that end, too.

The first method of slicing the cucumber is on the bias. Simply hold the cucumber at a 45 degree angle to the knife and slice it into thin slices.

Second, just slice it into circles. Turn the cucumber to a 90 degree angle and just start slicing.

Eggplant

Eggplant is one of those vegetables that is not used very often. I love it. It's a great vegetarian option since it has a soft billowy texture somewhat similar to chicken and can serve as a substitute for that meat.

Cut the ends off the eggplant.

Cut the eggplant in half widthwise to make it more manageable.

Peel the outer skin off with either a knife or a vegetable peeler. I like to use a knife because I find it easier and faster.

Once the skin is off, notice the little brown seeds throughout the white flesh. These seeds do not need to be removed since they are so small.

Garlic

Garlic can be messy to work with as it is sticky and has a very strong scent. It great when used with onions in soups and sauces.

First, peel off each individual clove from the bunch and use your knife to quickly smash it. This loosens the papery outside skin and makes it easier to peel off.

Next, cut off the tip and discard. Do this with all of the cloves you will be using.

Dice the garlic into small pieces. Keep the pieces very small because it's so strong that you don't want it to overpower the other ingredients in your soup, sauce or whatever you're making. Also it prevents you from biting into a big chunk of the potent material.

Green Beans

Green beans may be prepared by washing and removing both ends.

Herbs, Parsley

Parsley and other herbs may be used as a flavoring as well as a garnish.

Most fresh herbs are prepared by taking the leaves off the stem and cutting, or "mincing," them into extremely small pieces.

At this point, if you are going to use the herbs in a recipe, you're finished with the preparation and may add them to your mix. But if you're going to use them as a garnish, it's a good idea to dry them out, especially parsley.

Use your knife to put the "minced" pieces onto a paper towel or napkin.

Fold the paper towel or napkin around the particles and press down. The towel absorbs the moisture in the parsley and makes it much more flaky and spreadable.

Lettuce

Lettuce comes in many different varieties. It is used as the main ingredient in salads and as a topping on sandwiches.

It's important to know how to properly cut lettuce.

Slice the lettuce head, starting at the top and working down to the stem.

At this point, you can serve the lettuce immediately. If you're

storing it for use at a later time, then continue on to the next steps.

Take the cut lettuce and place it on a paper towel.

Fold the towel around the lettuce and press down. This will absorb excess moisture.

Place the lettuce in a Ziplock bag and remove any excess air. With the excess water gone and no air able to get in, the lettuce will keep much longer.

Melons/Cantaloupe

Most melons are cleaned the same way. Cut off the outside and scrape out the seeds. The technique demonstrated is universal for most melons and may be used for, Honeydew, Juan Canary melons, Crenshaw, etc.

Cut off the ends to create even surfaces for the melon to sit on so it doesn't roll around, making it more manageable and easier to cut.

Run the knife along the outside of the melon, removing the touch skin. Make sure to remove all the skin so that all you have left is the soft interior. If you don't want to take the time to remove the skin, simply skip this step and move to cleaning out the interior of the melon. Then use a spoon to remove the soft interior flesh from the shell. Many people like to do this if they are going to eat the melon directly from the shell.

Cut the melon in half lengthwise or widthwise.

Gently remove the seeds with a large spoon.

To slice the melon, hold the cleaned halves vertically and cut off strips of the melon.

To dice the melon, turn those cut strips and cut them into smaller chunks.

Mushrooms

Mushrooms are one vegetable that you do not want to wash before you start, since washing them can take away their natural flavor. To clean them, simply wipe them with a damp cloth.

Mushrooms are generally used in conjunction with other vegetables and ingredients like onion and garlic, not usually by themselves.

You may want to remove the stem which generally will just pop out with a slight twist. This makes the mushroom easier to work with. It doesn't have to be removed, in fact I usually don't remove the stem unless I am going to put some kind of stuffing or filling in its place.

Slicing mushrooms may be done by holding onto the end and slicing from the opposite side with the core intact or without.

Onions, Green or Scallions

Of all the different onions, green onions or scallions, require the least amount of work to clean and prepare.

Simply slice the green portion of the onions as thin as you like.

Slice the onions all the way through the white part, leaving off the stem, Most people use green onions as more of a garnish, that's why they stick to using the green portion predominately.

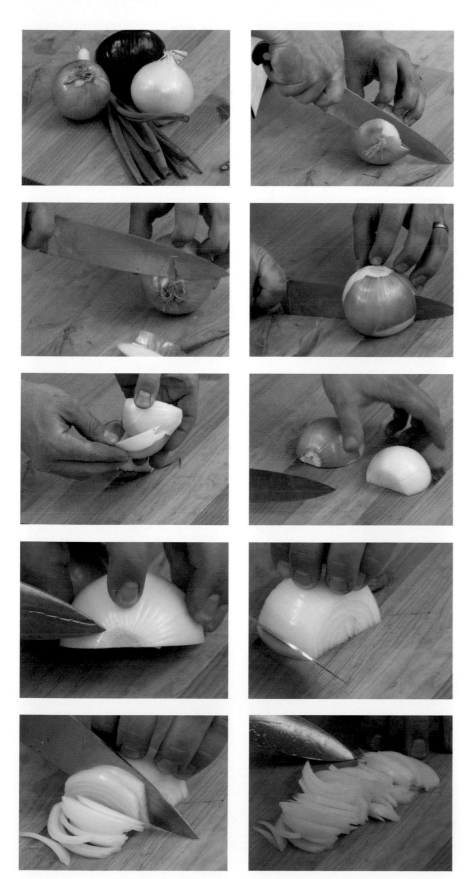

Onions—Yellow, White & Red

Yellow, white and red onions are all similar in size and taste. Red onions tend to be a little sweeter and are used in many dishes over the yellow or white ones because of their color. Yellow onions are most commonly used because they are the least expensive. Since the different varieties are all so similar, you can prepare them all the same way. Onions go well as a base vegetable for soups and sauces and are often paired with garlic and/or mushrooms.

Slicing or Julienning

Cut the top and bottom off.

At this point, you can either peel the skin off or you can cut the onion in half lengthwise, making it easier to take off the outside layers.

With the onion peeled, slice it as thin or as thick as you want.

Or dice the onion by turning the slices and dicing them into small pieces.

Dicing

Cut the top and bottom off just as you would if you were slicing or julienning the onion, except leave a little bit of the onion core on to help hold it together as you are dicing it.

Start by slicing the onion with your knife horizontal. Do not cut all the way through. Leave some of the onion intact to help hold it together.

Next, cut it similar to how you would if you were slicing it, except do not cut it all the way through.

Now that you have sliced it horizontally and vertically, you're ready to dice it. By leaving a portion of the onion intact, you may now cut it into uniform pieces and not make such a mess.

Be sure to remove the core that has helped you hold the onion together while slicing it.

Pineapple

Start by cutting off the bottom of the pineapple so that it will stand on its own as you cut off the top and sides.

After the sides are trimmed off, you will have what most people think is usable, however the middle of the pineapple is the actual "pine" which has a tough woody texture. To remove this part simply quarter the sheared column and then cut off the center.

Now slice up that golden goodness without the worry of biting into the woody, chewy part. When serving the pineapple, I like to include the top as a show piece (see photo).

Potatoes, Red

Red potatoes are very easy to clean because they are generally cooked with the skin on.

They may simply be cut in half, boiled and mashed.

Quarter the potatoes by cutting the halves in half and use them for roasting.

They may even be sliced for use as a breakfast potato or hash brown by simply slicing up the half. This way the potato doesn't move too much while you're cutting it.

Butternut Squash

Butternut squash is another versatile vegetable. Commonly used in soups, served roasted or mashed, butternut squash is truly a sweet and savory delight.

First, cut off the top and bottom.

When cleaning a butternut squash it helps to cut it into a more manageable size by cutting just above the circular base.

Peel the outside hard shell of the squash off of the circular portion and stem portion.

Next, cut the circular portion in two equal halves and take a large spoon and hollow out the seeds and stringy material inside. After the seeds have been removed, cut up the usable portion of this part of the squash.

Now take the stem portion of the squash and cut it in half lengthwise.

Do the same thing one more time by cutting the two sides in half lengthwise.

Turn the four pieces so that you can cut them into large dices. Butternut squash is very dense and hard in comparison to other vegetables. By cutting it into smaller pieces, it allows the pieces to cook much faster.

Squash, Spaghetti

Spaghetti squash is very unique. The reason it is called "spaghetti" is because it looks like spaghetti noodles when it is cooked. It is also unique in that you don't peel the outside off, you peel the inside out.

First, cut off the top and bottom. Then cut the squash lengthwise in two equal halves.

Take a large spoon and hollow out the seeds and loose stringy particles.

Now that the unusable parts have been removed, the next step is boiling or steaming the squash. This allows the "spaghetti-like" flesh to become loosened. This usually takes about 10 to 15 minutes. After the flesh is partly cooked, or blanched, peel out the "spaghetti" flesh.

At this point, you can either serve the squash or cool it down and store it to serve later. This happens commonly in restaurants where the squash is cooled only to be heated it up and serve later in combination with other veggies like broccoli, asparagus, carrots, etc.

Zucchini & Yellow Squash

Zucchini is another very versatile vegetable. Not only is it a great ingredient in sautéed vegetables, but it can be used in baking to make things like zucchini bread.

To clean zucchini for use in sautéed vegetables, cut off the ends, slice the zucchini lengthwise and then cut in quarter-inch slices. Since yellow squash is so similar to zucchini, use the same preparation procedure.

Tomato

Tomatoes come in many shapes and sizes. Pictured is a regular and a Roma tomato. The regular tomato is described as a 5x5 or 5x6 tomato because of how it is packaged. For example, a 5x5 (pronounced five-by-five) tomato is larger because it fits five long and five across in a box. The 5x6 is obviously smaller since they sit five long and six across. These tomatoes are commonly used as sandwich slices and wedges for salads.

Roma tomatoes are long and football shaped. They are almost always the cheapest and because of this are used for making salsas, soups and recipes that call for tomatoes in a cooked or diced form.

Other tomatoes include cherry tomatoes, grape tomatoes, beefsteak tomatoes, etc. Tomatoes also come in different colors as well, including yellow and orange. They all taste much the same. The only difference is they look different.

To prepare the tomato, remove the green stem.

To slice a tomato, slice off the top from where the stem was removed and simply continue slicing.

To dice the tomato, then turn the fruit and cut it lengthwise in half Cut each side in half one more time. Now you can put the two sides of one half of the tomato back together and turn the fruit and can cut it into smaller dices.

Yams

Yams are a very unique starch, in fact they are actually closer to a vegetable than a starch.

First peel the outside skin off of the yam using a vegetable peeler.

Cut the yam in half lengthwise.

Quarter the yam by cutting the halves in half and then dice as shown. This is the easiest way to prepare yams to use for mashing or for roasting, two favorite ways of preparing them.

Yearly vegetable availability

	Jan	Feb	Mar	Apr	May	Jun	Jul	Aug	Sep	Oct	Nov	Dec
Artichokes	Fair	Fair	Fair	Best	Best	Best	Good	Best	Best	Good	Fair	Fair
Asparagus	Good	Best	Best	Best	Best	Best	Fair	Fair	Best	Best	Fair	Fair
Beans	Good	Best	Good	Best	Best	Best	Best	Fair	Fair	Best	Best	Best
Beets	Good	Good	Best	Good	Good	Good	Best	Good	Good	Good	Good	Good
Chilli Peppers	Good	Good	Best	Best	Best	Best	Best	Best	Good	Good	Good	Good
Corn	Fair	Fair	Fair	Best	Best	Best	Best	Best	Good	Best	Fair	Good
Eggplant	Best	Best	Best	Best	Best	Best	Good	Good	Good	Best	Best	Best
Green Onions	Best	Best	Best	Best	Best	Best	Best	Good	Good	Good	Best	Best
Fresh Herbs	Good	Good	Good	Good	Good	Good	Good	Good	Good	Good	Good	Good
Jicama	Best	Best	Best	Best	Best	Best	Good	Good	Good	Good	Good	Good
Leeks	Best	Good	Good	Good	Best	Best	Best	Good	Good	Good	Best	Best
Onion–Red, White & Yellow	Good	Good	Best	Best	Best	Best	Best	Best	Best	Best	Best	Best
Peas	Good	Good	Good	Good	Best	Best	Best	Best	Fair	Fair	Fair	Fair
Potatoes	Best	Best	Best	Best	Best	Best	Best	Good	Good	Best	Best	Best
Radishes	Best	Best	Best	Good	Good	Good	Good	Good	Best	Good	Best	Best
Spinach	Good	Good	Good	Best	Best	Best	Best	Best	Best	Best	Best	Best
Squash	Best	Best	Best	Good	Good	Good	Best	Best	Best	Best	Best	Best
Sweet Potatoes	Good	Good	Best	Best	Good	Best	Best	Best	Best	Best	Best	Best
Turnips	Good	Good	Good	Good	Good	Good	Fair	Fair	Good	Good	Good	Good

	Best		Good		Fair		None

Vegetables that are always available:

Bell Peppers, Broccoli, Cabbage, Carrots, Cauliflower, Celery, Cucumbers, Garlic, Lettuce, Mushrooms

Yearly fruit availability

	Jan	Feb	Mar	Apr	May	Jun	Jul	Aug	Sep	Oct	Nov	Dec
Apricots	Fair	Fair	Fair	Best	Best	Best	Best	Fair	None	None	Fair	Fair
Blackberries	Good	Good	Good	Fair	Fair	Good	Best	Best	Good	None	Good	Good
Blueberries	Good	Good	Good	Fair	Fair	Best	Best	Best	Good	Good	Fair	Good
Cantaloupe	Good	Good	Good	Best	Best	Best	Best	Best	Best	Best	Good	Good
Cherries	None	None	None	None	Fair	Best	Best	Fair	None	None	None	None
Cranberries	None	None	None	None	None	None	None	None	Best	Best	Best	Fair
Figs	None	None	None	None	None	None	Good	Good	Best	Best	Good	None
Grapefruit	Best	Best	Best	Best	Best	Best	Good	Good	Good	Best	Best	Best
Grapes	Best	Best	Best	Good	Good	Best	Best	Best	Best	Best	Good	Best
Honeydew	Good	Good	Good	Good	Good	Best	Best	Best	Best	Best	Good	Good
Kiwi	Best	Best	Best	Best	Best	Best	Best	Fair	Fair	Best	Best	Best
Mangos	Good	Good	Good	Best	Best	Best	Best	Best	Good	Good	Fair	None
Nectarines	Fair	Fair	Fair	None	Fair	Good	Best	Best	Best	Fair	None	None
Oranges	Best	Best	Best	Best	Best	Best	Good	Best	Best	Best	Best	Best
Papaya	Good	Good	Good	Good	Good	Good	Good	Good	Good	Good	Good	Good
Peaches	Fair	Fair	None	None	Good	Best	Best	Best	Best	Fair	None	None
Pears	Best	Best	Best	Best	Good	Good	Fair	Best	Best	Best	Best	Best
Pineapples	Good	Best	Best	Best	Best	Best	Best	Best	Best	Best	Best	Good
Plums	Good	Good	Good	None	Good	Best	Best	Best	Best	Best	None	Good
Raspberries	None	None	Fair	Good	Fair	Good	Best	Best	Good	Fair	Good	Good
Strawberries	Fair	Fair	Good	Best	Best	Best	Best	Best	Best	Best	Fair	Good
Tangerines	Good	Good	Good	Fair	None	None	None	None	None	Good	Good	Good
Tomatoes, cherry	Good	Good	Good	Fair	Best	Best	Best	Best	Best	Best	Good	Good
Watermelon	None	Good	Best	Best	Best	Best	Best	Best	Best	Best	Good	Fair

	Best		Good		Fair		None

Fruits that are always available:

Apples, Avocado, Bananas, Lemons, Limes, Tomatoes

Chapter 10
Breading

A way to add a unique flavor and texture, as well as keep moisture in, is to bread your items. Whether it is beef, chicken, potatoes or vegetables, this technique is a great way to liven up a dish.

Step 1

Get the ingredients together—flour, eggs and bread crumbs.

Step 2

Put the flour in a pan or onto a plate and add some salt and pepper to season the flour.

Step 3

Crack the eggs into a bowl, discarding the shells, and beat them into a nice even mixture.

Step 4

Purchase pre-made bread crumbs at the grocery. They're available in many different sizes which saves considerable time and hassle, or make your own by drying out some bread and then crushing it up until it is the desired size. Put the crumbs into a pan or onto a plate similar to what you did with the flour. You may also add some salt and pepper, or any other desired seasoning, to the bread crumbs to give them a little more flavor.

Step 5

Take your item and coat it entirely with the flour, then dip it into the egg and finally in the bread crumbs. The flour helps the egg to stick and the egg holds the bread crumbs on.

Step 6

At this point, you may either fry or grill the item to seal the breading on. It all depends on what you are doing with it and what you like. For example, if I'm making chicken fingers, I will deep fry them, mostly because items with more of a round form like those thick chicken strips, carrots, zucchini, etc. are easier to cook that way. But if the item is flat such as a chicken breast, I'll just grill it.

In some cases, if you don't have enough breading on an item, you can always repeat the first five steps in the same process and double bread your item before deep frying or grilling.

Step 7

After cooking the outside of the breaded item, the inside may not always be done completely. If this is the case, then place the item(s) on a sheet or roasting pan and finish cooking it in the oven.

Chapter 11
Cooking Pasta, Potatoes or Rice

An integral part of every meal is the starch. Potatoes, rice and pasta all make up this realm. Even though there are others, these are the ones most people commonly use.

Pasta

There are a lot of different kinds of pasta but really only one way to cook it—with moist heat, and more specifically, by boiling. Here is a quick run down on pastas and what I usually use them for.

Types of pasta: rotelli, penne, spaghetti, vermicelli, linguine, angel hair or cappellini, shells (large and small), rigatoni, fettuccine, and egg noodles (large, medium and small).

The pasta pieces such as the rotelli, pasta shells or the penne I use to capture the sauce. So if it's a tomato sauce, the pasta pieces act like little buckets and pick up and hold the sauce better than the strands, such as the fettuccine or spaghetti. The pasta strands are used in dishes that have a thicker sauce, such as Alfredo, and bigger items such as meatballs or chicken.

Some people might ask about the difference between hard noodles (store-bought, in-the-box kind) and soft noodles (homemade or fresh). My answer in the simplest way I know how to say it is, the softer the noodle, the faster it cooks. And that's about it. In other words, homemade noodles cook in about half the time, although you follow the same procedure for both.

Step 1

Get the water boiling.

Fill a pot with at least twice the water as you have pasta and put it on the stove. Make sure you use the warmest water that will come from your tap because that will cut your heating time drastically. Then turn it on high until it boils. Keep in mind the water needs to be brought to a boil before you go to the next step. This will ensure the best results.

Homemade noodles cook in about half the time of packaged noodles, although you follow the same procedure for both.

Step 2

Drop in the pasta.

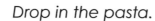

After the water is boiling, just drop the pasta in.

When you take pasta out of the package, it's usually pretty long. So a good way to get it to fit into any pot is to break it. That's right, not only does it make the pasta more manageable, it also cuts down on the cooking time since the pasta is smaller. The same applies when you're cooking some rotelli or pasta shells.

When working with spaghetti or any longer noodle, break the long pasta strands in half so they fit better in the pan.

Step 3

Stir, stir, stir.

Stir the pasta. Why? Because pasta will stick to the bottom of the pan, the sides and the other pieces of pasta, so stir the pasta at least every 30 seconds or so.

Step 4

Cook it until it's done.

So when is pasta done? You may have heard that it's done when you can throw a piece against the wall and it sticks. You can try that, but this method has never really worked for me and wouldn't you rather just be able to tell by tasting it and feeling the texture? Of course you would. So just remember this—*firm* is the key, not crunchy because then it's underdone. And not mushy because then it's overdone. This cooking process usually only takes about five to ten minutes, depending on how much and what kind of pasta you are cooking.

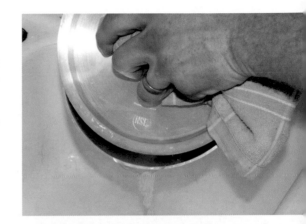

Step 5

Drain it.

This is where your colander comes into play. Simply dump the water and pasta into the colander or strainer and let all that hot water out, leaving you with your perfectly cooked pasta.

Another way I like to drain water out of pots and pans is to simply use the lid. I just hold the lid firmly on the top with a small space to allow the water to drain out. This way I don't dirty another dish.

Be careful when using these draining methods as the steam that comes off of this mix can leave a nasty burn. It's a good idea to always use dry towels or hot pads when doing this.

So what happens when you cook the pasta just right, take it out of the water and let it sit and cool for a minute it, and all of the sudden it turns out overdone? This leads to the next step. Remember carry-over cooking?

Step 6

Shock and oil.

Since pasta is cooked at such high temperatures, it takes longer for it to cool down, making the carry-over cooking time longer. So remember to shock and oil, since cooking it perfectly is only half the battle.

To shock the pasta, run cold water over it as soon as it is drained. This cools the pasta down and stops the cooking process so that the pasta stays firm and doesn't go mushy.

After you stop the cooking process, simply add some oil to the pasta, stirring it throughout the noodles so that they are all coated. This keeps the pasta from sticking and makes it more manageable. Not a lot of oil is needed, however the amount of oil will vary depending on what kind and how much pasta is being served. I usually use about one teaspoon per serving. So if you're making pasta for ten people, about two tablespoons should work just fine. Remember you're just adding enough oil so that the noodles don't stick together. Experiment and see what works for you.

This is crucial, especially when it comes to making pasta salads. You obviously don't want people "crunching" through the salad and getting clumps of noodles because the pasta is sticky from either not being cooked enough or being overdone.

Serving it hot

If you're serving the pasta hot, then shocking it is not necessary since you'll just have to heat it up again. For this, just mixing the oil into it should do. Just make sure you serve it as soon as possible to ensure the best results.

Add some oil to the pasta to coat the noodles so they don't stick and are more manageable.

Potatoes

Of all of the starches, potatoes are probably the most versatile and also the most diverse. There are a lot of different kinds of potatoes, but the principles of cooking them are the same no matter what kind you're using. The different kinds allow for different uses and are best utilized for certain uses. For example, you don't use a fingerling potato for mashed potatoes, simply because they are more expensive and you get fewer yields out of them. Or in other words, you get more bang for your buck by using certain types for certain recipes.

So what are the different types of potatoes and what are they used for?

Let's start backwards. When determining what kind of potato to use, decide how you want to prepare it. This will help you narrow down the choices dramatically.

Cooking Method	Potatoes	Advantages	Disadvantages
Mashed	*Reds*	Don't have to skin, makes unique dish with red skins mixed in	If you do skin them, it takes a lot longer
	Yukon Gold	Don't have to skin, nice gold color. Good yield, easy	If you do skin them, it takes a lot longer
	Finglering		Smaller potato, not a very good yield
	Russets	Cheapest, larger so you get a better yield, most used	
	Yams/Sweet Potatoes	Unique orange color and flavor	

Roasted	*Reds*	Unique red skin color, don't have to cut as much since they are already small	
	Yukon Gold	Unique gold color, don't have to cut as much since they are already small and pretty	
	Fingerling	Smaller, more petite appearance, don't have to cut down to size	
	Russets	Good yield, more product for your money	Larger, requires more cutting and cleaning
	Yams/Sweet potatoes	Don't have to pre-cook, nice unique color and flavor	

Baked	Reds		Small, longer to prepare and cook
	Yukon Gold		Small, longer to prepare and cook
	Fingerling		Small, longer to prepare and cook
	Russets	Largest, best yield, cheapest	
	Yams/Sweet potatoes	Unique color, flavor, large, good yield	

Mashed Potatoes
The Art of Cut, Cook and Smash!

This is probably the most common method of cooking potatoes, as well as being probably the most worry-free since you can't really overdo them.

Step 1

Wash and scrub.

The preliminary step, no matter what method or type of potato you are cooking, is to wash them. Some people just wash them by running them under water, but I have found that a good scrubber is a must-have. Dirt likes to hide in the little crevices of the potato and a scrubber helps to dig it out.

Step 2

Cut up the potato.

Since you'll probably be using russets most of the time, and even if you're using reds or a smaller potato, cut them down to decrease the cooking time. It's a lot faster to heat four or five smaller pieces than one big piece.

Step 3

Cook the potatoes.

Put the cut-up potatoes in a pot and add just enough water to barely cover them. Then put the pot on the stove, turn the temperature to high so that the water will boil, then walk away for about 30 minutes. That's right, just walk away and let them cook until they fall apart.

Overdoing mashed potatoes is not really an option, although it can be done. Unless you are going to leave the potatoes in boiling water for two hours, you can't overcook them. Undercooking them is a different story. How you can tell if they're undercooked? You'll have chunky pieces of potatoes instead of that nice, thick, creamy texture. As I said before, cook them until they fall apart.

Step 4

Get your liquid mix hot.

Once you have the potatoes heating on the stove, it's time to get your liquid mix of butter and milk going. This is what you mix in with your potatoes when they are all done and drained to give them that nice creamy texture. This way, the mix will be hot when you're ready to add it to the cooked potatoes. By doing this, you keep the potatoes hot instead of putting a lukewarm or cold liquid in the potatoes, bringing the temperature down dramatically.

Depending on how many potatoes you're cooking, about 1½ cups of milk and ¼ pound of butter to five large, russet potatoes is a good mix. You can also use water or any other liquid mixture if you like. It really depends on how you like the consistency of your mashed potatoes as to how much liquid you put in.

Step 5

Drain and mash the potatoes.

After the potato is cooked to the point that it falls apart when you touch it, then you're ready to mash them.

Start by draining the water from the potatoes just as you would with pasta. Then add the hot milk and butter mixture. Use a whisk or a hand mixer, aka egg beater. Once again, try both and decide what you like best. You might decide that you like using a spoon. That's alright. It's your kitchen.

Mix the liquid into the potatoes until the mix is a consistent texture throughout. Add some salt and pepper to your liking (and you're set.

No Mess Tip

When using a mixer, chances are you'll probably make a mess. A good way to prevent this is to put some plastic wrap around the mixer/egg beater and the bowl so that it doesn't spray all over the kitchen.

Leave the skin on the potato unless it's a sweet potato or yam.

Making Unique Mashed Potatoes

After your potatoes are mixed, you can leave them as they are or you can take my advice and make them unique. One of my favorite things to do is add things to my mashed potatoes to make them unique such as cheddar cheese, blue cheese, garlic, bacon and anything else that I might like. This is the nice thing about potatoes and cooking in general. Once you learn a few of the basics, you can do whatever you want. I've even seen chefs put things like corn, mushrooms and onions in mashed potatoes, which goes to show that there really is no limit. If you like it, do it.

Roasting Potatoes and Cooking Potatoes for Potato Salad

I have found that the best way to perfectly roast potatoes is to combine the cooking methods of boiling and roasting.

When using this cooking method you can choose to peel the potato or not. If I'm roasting potatoes, I usually always leave the skin on, except with a sweet potato or yam. In my opinion, these are always better with the skin off.

Another advantage of using sweet potatoes and yams is that you don't need to pre-cook or blanch them. Cut them and skip the boiling and draining and go right to coating them.

Before starting these steps, make sure to preheat the oven and begin melting the butter so that these things are done when you're ready for them.

When cooking potatoes for cold dishes like potato salad, simply follow the first three steps.

Step 1

Cut them.

The difference between cutting potatoes used for roasting and potatoes used for mashing is consistency. When making mashed potatoes, it doesn't matter if one is slightly bigger or smaller than the others because they're going to get mashed anyway. But when it comes to roasted potatoes, when you cut the potato, that's what the finished product is going to look like. So being consistent is more important when it comes to this cooking method for presentation and also for getting the best product. Don't cut one too big and leave others small because then the small ones come out perfectly and the big one comes out crunchy since it takes longer for the bigger pieces to cook.

Step 2

Boil them.

Just like mashed potatoes, put them in the water and get it boiling. But unlike mashed potatoes, you can easily overcook them. The purpose of precooking or blanching, a fancy term for pre-cooking, is to prevent overcooking. We just want to get the cooking process started, not cook them all the way. This way, they'll have a nice texture and color on the outside when we roast them but still be soft on the inside. Without boiling them, you would have to practically burn them on the outside to get a soft inside.

When the potatoes are finished boiling they should still be firm but not rock-hard. The inside color will start to look different, more of an off-white, translucent color. The whole process usually only takes about five minutes of boiling to get them to this point.

Step 3

Drain & shock them.

Now that your potatoes are precooked or blanched, it's time to drain them and shock them.

Why shock the potatoes? The same reason as shocking pasta and vegetables—to stop cooking. This also makes the potatoes easier to work with when we go to the next step of coating them. This step is the key when it comes to making potato salad. It enables you to actually make potato *salad*, instead of what some call potato salad but actually tastes more like mashed potatoes and mayo, which is what happens when the potatoes are overdone.

Drain the water just as you would when doing pasta or vegetables. The shock the potatoes, again like you would with the pasta or vegetables. The principles and methods are the same. As I said in the beginning, once you learn what cooking is all about and why we do what we do, you can make just about anything.

Note: If you're making potato salad, simply mix your other ingredients in with your now perfectly cooked potatoes and that's it.

Step 4

Coat them.

When coating the potatoes, you're actually covering the outside with a thin layer of fat to help give it the taste and texture you want. I usually use butter, but you can use olive oil, canola oil, margarine, or any other fatty substance. Just know that it is through my experience of using everything else that I learned to stick with butter. You may have a different experience and prefer olive oil and that's alright, too— because it's your kitchen.

First, make sure the butter melted, if that's what you're going to use. Pour the fat into a mixing bowl, add your spices, and then add the precooked potatoes. Mix everything with clean hands, preferably with gloves since it's kind of messy. Use a large spoon instead if you don't feel comfortable diving in with your hands.

After each potato is sufficiently coated, pour the entire bowl onto the pan and spread it out evenly.

Step 5

Roast them.

Now, after all that work, you finally get to put them in the oven. Set the temperature to 350 degrees and slide the pan in, preferably on the middle or top shelf, so that the bottom doesn't burn, Most of the time it won't, but putting it up a shelf just helps to make sure.

Depending on what type of potato you're using, it may take up to forty-five minutes to an hour to cook. The potatoes are done when they have a nice golden brown skin and soft texture.

Baked Potatoes

This is by far the easiest, least time-consuming way to cook potatoes. Even though baked potatoes actually involve two cooking methods just like the roasted potatoes, the bakers do the first step for you because they actually steam themselves while they are being baked. So when you put the potato in the oven, the heat from the oven heats up the outside while the moisture inside the potato heats up the inside.

Cook potatoes at 350 degrees. Most of the time, cooking potatoes this way can take anywhere from forty-five minutes to an hour to cook, depending on the size. When it comes to baking potatoes, you actually only have to do one step. Just choose which way you want to bake them and follow that step.

Step 1

Microwaving cuts the baking time down significantly.

If you have large potatoes, they can take a very long time to cook in the oven. I like to get them started by putting them in the microwave for three to five minutes, depending on the size, so that the actual baking time is less. Five minutes in the microwave can save you thirty minutes in the oven.

If you don't have time to bake the potato in the oven, you can actually cook it all the way in the microwave if necessary. Depending on the size, the smaller ones may only take five minutes total.

Step 2

Poking holes in the skin will prevent the potato from exploding.

If you choose not to wrap your potatoes in foil, they can and do explode from time to time. Trust me, this is not fun to clean up, especially since potatoes have a tendency to streak and smear instead of just coming off nice and easy. The benefit to poking holes is that it gives the potato a chance to "let off some steam" that builds up inside. That way the potato doesn't explode.

Preparing the Potatoes

Step 1

Coated.

Coat the potatoes with butter or whatever fat or oil you like. Put them in the oven, preferably on a sheet or pan of some sort so that it doesn't get your oven messy.

Step 2

Wrapped.

Simply wrap the potato in foil and put it in the oven right on the rack. A pan is not necessary. Before I wrap potatoes with foil, I like to coat them because it gives the skin a nice texture.

Step 3

Crispy.

Simply throw the potato in the oven. That's it. This is my personal favorite because of how easy it is to prepare and because of how the potato turns out. I like the crunchiness of the skin. You can also hollow it out and just eat the skin plain.

When the potatoes are done, they will feel soft, but still somewhat firm, and the insides will be soft and billowy.

Topping the Potatoes

Much like mashed potatoes, you can add anything you like to top a baked potato.

These are just some of the things that I have seen and used.

- Broccoli and Cheese Sauce
- Gravy—brown, white, etc.
- Cheese—cheddar, mozzarella, etc.
- Butter
- Sour Cream
- Green Onions or Chives
- Bacon Pieces or Bacon Bits
- Diced Ham
- Chili
- Sautéed Mushrooms

Rice

Like pasta, there are a lot of different kinds of rice. To make it easier, I will focus on the two primary types—white rice and brown rice.

White rice is the most common type of rice used today. Most food service outlets, restaurants and homes use white rice, mainly because it's cheap and cooks the quickest.

But when you think about a healthy starch, brown rice is at the top of the list. Although it's not used as much as white rice, it is growing in popularity even though it takes a lot longer to cook than white rice.

Cooking Rice

Whether it's white or brown, cooking rice is a simple process that follows the moist cooking method of simmering. You may also bake rice in the oven.

Simmering Rice

Step 1

Measure the rice, measure the water.

The ratio of rice to water or liquid is two to one. So when you're cooking rice, make sure that if you have one cup of rice, you put in two cups of water.

This is almost always the case unless you're cooking what is known as parboiled rice. Parboiled rice is simply rice that has been precooked so that the cooking time is much less. If you're using parboiled rice, be sure to follow the instructions on the package. If there are no instructions, then the ratio is generally 1½ to 1 instead of the regular two to one.

Step 2

Combine and cook.

Combine the rice and the water in a pot and place it on the stove. I usually set the temperature at 50 to 75 percent on the dial so that it heats quickly but doesn't burn on the bottom.

Depending on the amount of rice and what kind it is (brown rice takes longer than parboiled or white rice), the rice will take anywhere from twenty to forty-five minutes to cook. When it's done, it will be soft and almost, if not all, of the water in the pot, will have been absorbed into the rice.

When cooking rice remember the ratio of rice to water or liquid is two to one—one cup of rice to two cups of water.

Sticky Rice

If you want sticky rice, simply stir the rice and water while it is cooking. This is harder with brown rice but can still be done.

Baking

Step 1

Measure the rice, measure the water.

This is the same as Step 1 on simmering the rice.

Step 2

Combine and cook.

Combine the rice and the water in an oven-proof pan. Preheat the oven, setting the temperature at 350 degrees, then cover the pan with foil and place it in the oven.

Depending on the amount of rice and what kind it is (brown rice takes longer than parboiled or white), it will take anywhere from thirty to sixty minutes to cook. When it is done, it will be soft and almost all of the water in the pan will have been absorbed into the rice.

> ### Tips for making rice unique
> **When I make rice, whether for myself or for anyone else, I want it to be flavorful. So instead of using just water, I will use some kind of seasoned liquid—most of the time chicken broth. Through the years, I have found that this tastes the best to me.**

Just as there are a lot of different kinds of rice, there are also a lot of different ways of preparing it. By adding a few simple ingredients you can make your own favorite recipes.

Additions	Dish	Notes
Tomato sauce, onion	Spanish rice	
Soy sauce, egg, carrots, onions, bean sprouts	Fried rice	Add ham for "ham-fried rice", shrimp for "shrimp-fried rice," etc.
Onion, carrot, celery	Rice pilaf	Cook all ingredients together

These are just a few simple recipes and examples of dishes that you can create. With fried rice and Spanish rice, always cook the ingredients first, then add the cooked rice.

Chapter 12
Soups & Sauces

Soups and sauces require a certain level of knowledge and skill, but they aren't rocket science.

When people ask "what is your favorite thing to cook?" I readily answer "soups and sauces."

I've found that if you can make a good sauce or soup, you'll win over almost any crowd. Sauces provide a great way to mask things such as meat that isn't quite as tender or juicy as you want, or perhaps it just doesn't taste great and isn't that pretty. But they can also make a great product even better. For example, mashed potatoes are good, but mashed potatoes and gravy are much better.

Soups and sauces are one area of cooking that you will have to practice, practice, practice. They require a certain level of knowledge and skill, but as you will see, they aren't rocket science.

Before I jump right into sauces, let's make sure you understand what the two key ingredients are.

Stock

You may have heard some people call this broth. The easiest way is to buy it. You will usually find it in the canned soup area of the grocery store. It will generally come in flavors like beef and chicken. The beef you can use for dark gravies and sauces. The chicken you can use for light gravies or sauces.

Thickening agent

These are items or combinations of items that help thicken sauces. The two most common are roux and cornstarch. For simplicity I will focus on these two since they are the most common.

Roux

Roux *(pronounced roo)* is equal parts fat and flour. Now when I say equal parts, I mean by weight, not by volume. For example, if you have one cup of flour, it's going to weigh more than one cup of butter. So measure it according to weight.

Once again, I prefer to use butter but you can make your roux out of any fat you want. I sometimes like to use bacon grease.

When cooking roux, it's important to 1) cook it long enough and 2) cook it according to what you're making. For example, don't cook it so long that it turns a dark brown and then use it to make a nice, white colored soup like cream of broccoli. Why? Because even though you want to be able to see a light color and predominately taste creaminess, the roux will make the soup darker and give it a darker, more nutty taste. A dark roux does have its place in things like dark gravies and soups, but it's important to understand the what-and-how of cooking with roux so that you can determine what you need for what you are making.

How to Make Roux

First you need to get the fat into a liquid form. Second, add the flour to the melted fat and mix it thoroughly. Third, cook it. This is the most important part of any roux, both stirring it constantly and making sure you cook it long enough for what you're making. If you are making a dark sauce, you'll want to make the roux a little darker by cooking it a little longer and the same goes if you're making a lighter sauce. You'll cook it less.

How to Save Time and Get the Roux and Stock to Mix Perfectly

When mixing the roux in with the stock, or vice versa, many cooks run into the problem of getting little balls of roux that don't mix into the sauce. To avoid this and to help to cut down on your cooking time, cook the roux, set it aside in a storage container and use it as needed. That way you can heat up just the stock, then add the roux as needed. You don't have to cook a roux every time you make a sauce. This is what a lot of professional kitchens do to save time.

The key to not getting any of those little flour balls in your sauces is to remember this simple rule—hot stock and cold roux, or hot roux and cold stock. Now when I say cold, I don't mean that is has to be right out of the fridge; straight out of the can or at room temperature is fine. The same holds true with cold roux. Room temperature is just fine.

This little trick has saved me more than once. But just in case you still have those little flour clumps, run your sauce through a strainer just as you would when draining pasta or anything else.

Roux to Stock

I generally use about two cups of roux to every one gallon of stock. If you want your sauce thicker or thinner, simply add more or less roux.

Cornstarch

I prefer to make what you would call slurry, which is just water and cornstarch. Follow the instructions on the package. It will tell you to add a certain amount of water to the cornstarch. But I use the smallest amount of water which makes more of a paste. This allows the soup or sauce to which you're adding the slurry to thicken faster because you aren't adding as much liquid.

Blender/puree

You may also use a blender to puree whole ingredients which helps to thicken some mixtures. This is the thickening method I use for tomato sauce. This technique doesn't work the same as the roux or the cornstarch, but it has its place.

Mother Sauces

Did you know that every sauce you make will fall into one of five categories known as the Mother Sauces? When I tell you that by learning to make these five sauces you should be able to make just about any sauce, don't be surprised.

Below is a chart that shows the basic ingredients for these Mother Sauces.

Sauce	Basic Ingredients
Béchamel sauce or cream sauce	Milk, thickening agent
Veloute sauce or light gravy	Light stock, thickening agent
Tomato sauce	Tomatoes
Hollandaise sauce	Egg yolks, butter
Espagnol sauce or dark gravy	Dark stock, thickening agent

Deglazing

An important part of making soups or sauces is what is called deglazing.

When cooking your items in the pan, whether vegetables or some sort of meat, they caramelize when they cook. That means that natural sugars inside come out and usually turn brown. That's why when you grill an item you get that nice, brown color on the outside. Sometimes those sugars also stick to the pan. To get them off of the pan and into the sauce, you deglaze the pan. To do this, add a little bit of acid.

So before you add anything else, add something like a citrus juice such as lime or lemon juice, a wine or vinegar of some sort (red wine vinegar, apple cider vinegar). These are all examples of acids, but there are ingredients that you can use that have acid in them that you may not have thought of. Tomatoes have a lot of natural acid in them, so when I make a tomato-based sauce, I usually don't add a lot of extra acid, because I don't need to.

When making sauces, I recommend using wine or something with a more mild flavor so that it doesn't overpower the other flavors.

Béchamel Sauce

What is it?

This is the sauce in a creamy soup or a cheese sauce.

Examples

Cream soups like cream of mushroom or celery, cheese sauces, as well as cream sauces like pesto cream or scallion cream that you might see on restaurant menus.

How to make it

Use cream, milk, heavy cream, etc. like a stock and add the desired flavor to the cream.

Veloute Sauce

What is it?

This is usually a nice, light gravy.

Examples

Light gravies like turkey or chicken.

How to make it

The basic sauce is made by combining a light stock, such as poultry or fish, and a thickening agent, such as roux.

Tomato Sauce

What is it?

This sauce is made primarily of tomatoes which have been pureed, diced, or stewed, or tomato juice.

Examples

Marinara sauce is used for and in many Italian dishes. Also, as few people know, it is the mother sauce for the popular Oriental Sweet and Sour Sauce.

How to make it

The basic tomato sauce is just that, tomatoes. So depending on the sauce that you're making, by starting with a tomato product such as tomato puree, juice or canned tomato sauce, and then adding the other ingredients, you have the basic sauce down right from the start.

Hollandaise Sauce

What is it?

A very unique, rich buttery sauce made from egg yolks and butter.

Separate the egg white and the egg yolk

Get your water boiling and place a mixing bowl over the top

Examples

This is the sauce served on top of the popular breakfast dish, Eggs Benedict. As a side dish, Hollandaise is served on top of vegetables such as asparagus. Also by adding some sautéed shallots or onions, the sauce goes from a Hollandaise to a Béarnaise, a sauce popularly served on top of a steak, such as tenderloin.

How to make it

This is one of the more challenging sauces to accomplish. The sauce is made basically by combining warm egg yolks and melted butter. When combined, these two ingredients automatically thicken and do not require a thickening agent. The process of combining the egg and the fat or oil is called emulsification and is used in making other things like salad dressing and mayonnaise.

Espanol Sauce

What is it?

This is beef gravy..

Examples

Most beef sauces and gravies.

How to make it

This sauce is created by combining a brown stock, like beef, and a thickening agent, like roux. Begin by making a darker roux. Then add your beef stock or broth and stir until the mix is consistent throughout.

Slowly pour in the butter while whisking

Don't scramble it or overcook it

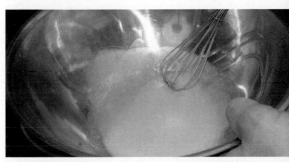

Look for a nice, even consistency

Melt the butter

Add the flour

Add the stock

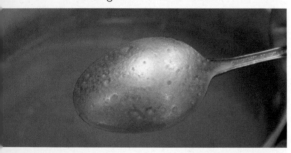

Stir together until smooth

Bad—too thin

Good

Some butter at the end adds a nice texture and flavor

One Pot Step-by-Step Sauce Making-Veloute, Béchamel, Espanol

Step 1

Get a sauce pot and place it on the stove. Turn the element on medium to high heat.

Step 2

Place the butter, or whatever fat or oil you're using, in the pot and allow the butter to melt completely.

Step 3

Add the appropriate amount of flour to the melted butter and mix together.

Step 4

Cook the mixture until it reaches the desired color, smell and texture. And remember, the darker the sauce, the darker the roux. So when you're making a béchamel use a light roux, a little darker roux for a Veloute, and a dark roux for a Espanol sauce.

This is the point where you may want to deglaze the pan by adding about a tablespoon of some sort of acid such as vinegar, citrus juice or wine.

Step 5

Add the desired stock. If you're making a darker sauce, use a darker stock (beef). For a light sauce, use a light stock (chicken).

Step 6

After you have added the stock, mix it together with the roux until it is consistently the same throughout. It may not look like it is as thick as you want it, but remember roux takes about twenty minutes of simmering to fully thicken.

Step 7

At this point, you can season the mix. Salt and pepper to taste usually is the best place to start. After seasoning the sauce, you're ready to serve.

Chapter 13
Seasoning

This is the fun part. Here is where you become the expert and where you get to make each dish your own.

Experimenting is the key. All new recipes and ideas come from someone trying something new, so go ahead and be a pioneer! The great part about it is that you can always fix it if you mess up.

Just so you know ahead of time, it's a good idea to know what the spices taste like before you start cooking. That means that you may need to taste everything, or at least what you want to use, beforehand so you know how to use it.

Getting the Best Herbs

- Grow your own. This is how you'll be able to get the best quality.

- Shop busy stores. Why? Because they move their inventory faster, which means fresher herbs.

- Don't buy herbs that are faded or off-color. Get bright, nice-looking herbs with little to no dark spots whenever possible.

Tips for Using Herbs

1. If you're substituting dry for fresh herbs, remember that dried herbs are stronger than fresh herbs, about three to one. So when you're adding dried herbs to a recipe that calls for fresh herbs, use a third of what you would have in the recipe.

2. When using dried herbs, crush them up in your hand before adding them. This actually helps release the flavor faster.

3. Use only one strong-flavored herb in a dish. For example, rosemary and sage are both very powerful and, although they can be mixed with other seasonings, they are usually very dominant. One strong seasoning can be combined with other more mild ones. Thyme, basil and oregano are all pretty strong independently, with oregano usually standing out; but together they are the perfect Italian seasoning. Whole herb leaves are a better choice than ground or powdered simply because they hold their flavor better and longer.

It's a good idea to know what the spices taste like before you start cooking.

Tips for Using Spices

1. When you're planning and executing your menu, remember to not season more than one dish in your meal with the same herb or spice. Also every dish on the menu does not need to be herbed or spiced. Salt and pepper are my best friends and they make for some great seasoning simply because they accentuate the natural flavors in the food without overpowering it.

2. If you're substituting whole spices for ground, then use about 1½ times as much as the recipe calls for. So if the recipe calls for two tablespoons of ground spice, but you only have whole, then measure three tablespoons of whole to compensate. This follows the same rules for increasing recipes in general.

Doubling or Cutting Down a Recipe

Remember that when doubling or cutting down a recipe to adjust seasonings accordingly.

When doubling a recipe, don't just automatically double the herbs and spices. Instead, add what the recipe calls for and then taste it and add more if necessary. This hlds true for cutting recipes down. Add just a little bit less than what you think, because you can always add more if it needs it and that's a lot easier than trying to take it away.

What has Worked for Others

There are some classic combinations and general spices that go well with each other and are often used in certain dishes.

Combinations

Salt and pepper—These are the all purpose spices used for virtually anything, to enhance rather than create flavors

Cinnamon and nutmeg—Used mostly in dessert items

Oregano, basil and thyme—Also known as the all-purpose Italian seasoning

Granulated garlic and onion, salt, pepper—Use this to season most meats, poultry, fish and potatoes. (It's kind of like my all-purpose spice so I can call it the "Chef Shawn spice.")

Cayenne pepper, chili powder, paprika, salt—A nice southwest spice to use when barbecuing items and a good, spicy steak seasoning, too.

Lemon pepper—Buy this at the grocery. It makes a great, unique seasoning for items such as vegetables and fish, instead of just using salt and regular pepper.

Pickling spice—Buy this at the grocery. It's usually a combination of bay leaves and whole peppercorns. This is a good spice which adds a unique flavor to add to the water when boiling shrimp or even beef or chicken.

Conclusion

Experiment! This is what cooking is all about—finding what works for you.

I have had dishwashers show me how to skin potatoes faster than any chef I ever worked for and I have had banquet servers show me how to cut lemons and limes more symmetrically and perfect than anyone working in the kitchen. If it works for you, then that's how you do it. Just remember that you can learn something from everyone. So even though something might work for you today, someone might show you an easier, faster way tomorrow. Keep an open mind and have fun!

From the Chef

As a chef, I get a lot of cooking questions. After a couple hundred of these, I found that I wished I had a book I could refer people to read. But I just didn't feel comfortable sending them to a monstrosity of a professional cookbook with a myriad of words that they wouldn't understand. Most books of this sort are really just collections of recipes anyway.

Since there was nothing on the market that I could refer people to, I decided to write my own. That's when *The First-Timer's Cookbook* series began to take shape. These books are for anyone who has ever, or never, stepped into a kitchen and wondered what to do. This is the first book which deals with all the basics of cooking. It will be the first book you buy, either for yourself, your kids, even your grandkids, and the book you'll compare all the others to.

I hope you enjoy it.

—Chef Shawn Bucher

Chef Bucher holds business degrees and a culinary certificate. He has worked in the food service industry for over twelve years from grocery stores to restaurants, hotels and schools, to corporate training and development.